BOOK 4

Grand Trios for Piano

4 EARLY INTERMEDIATE PIECES FOR ONE PIANO, SIX HANDS

Melody Bober

Trio playing is both energizing and exciting, and there are many ensemble possibilities: a teacher and two students; a parent and two siblings; or, my favorite, three friends. While performances can be thrilling, preparing trio music can be enjoyable as well since sharing the love of music with others is so rewarding.

Trios also offer a great musical experience for students. Rhythm, phrasing, articulation, and dynamics all become wonderful teaching tools while students learn to listen for that unique blending of parts. I have written *Grand Trios for Piano*, Book 4, so that today's piano students can experience music in a variety of styles, meters, and tempos. I have also written this collection so that students can progress technically and musically...together!

I sincerely hope that students will find the pieces challenging and fun in these *Grand Trios for Piano*!

Best wishes,

CONTENTS

Alfred

Alfred Music Publishing Co., Inc.
P.O. Box 10003
Van Nuys, CA 91410-0003
alfred.com

ISBN-10: 0-7390-7935-2
ISBN-13: 978-0-7390-7935-5

Cover Photos
stage lights: © stock.xchng/photos71

Harvest Time Rag

Melody Bober

Middle

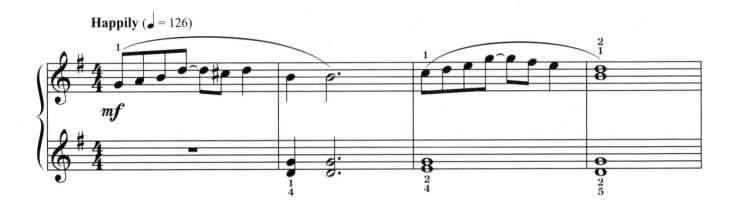

Low

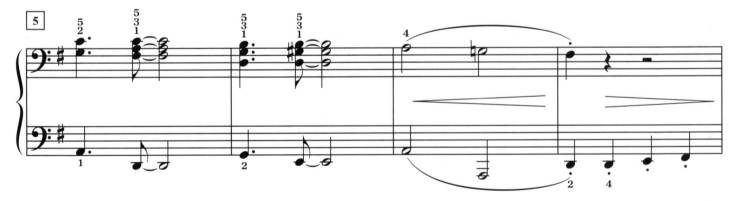

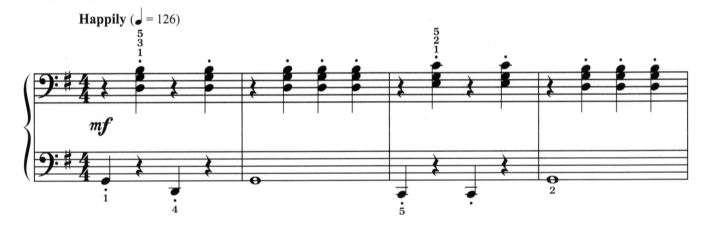

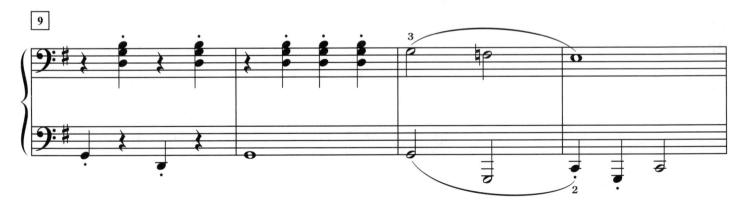

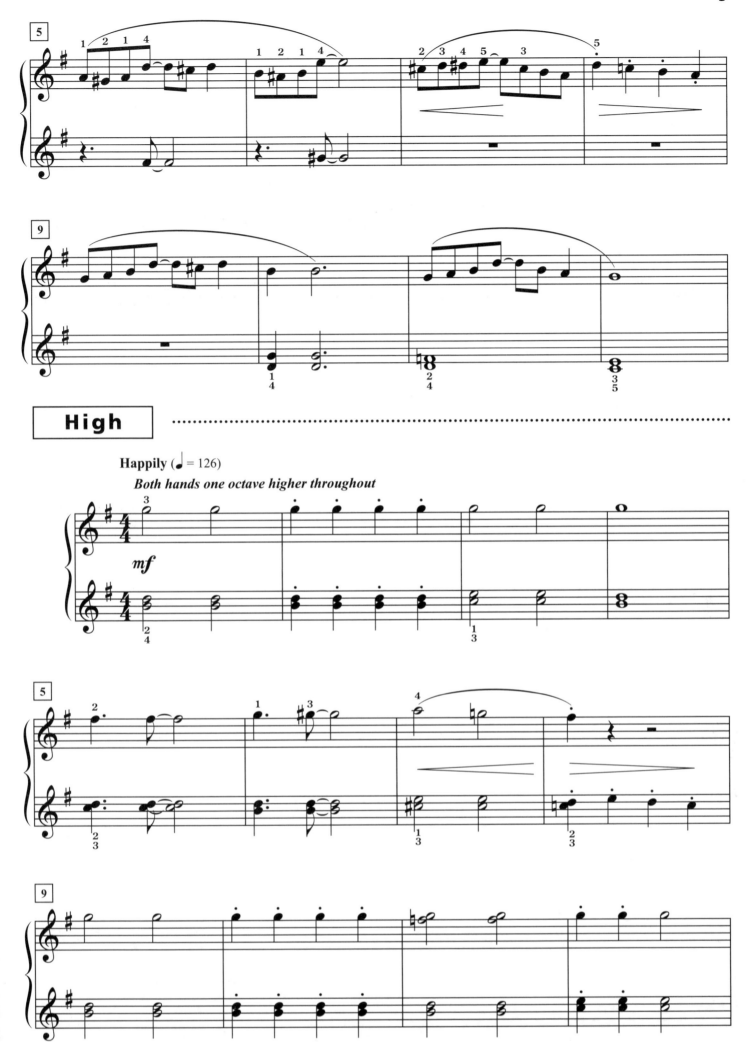

High

Happily (♩ = 126)

Both hands one octave higher throughout

mf

Middle

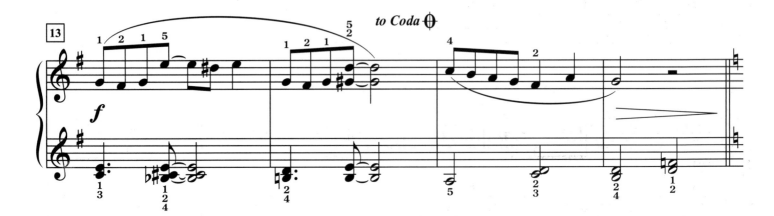

Low

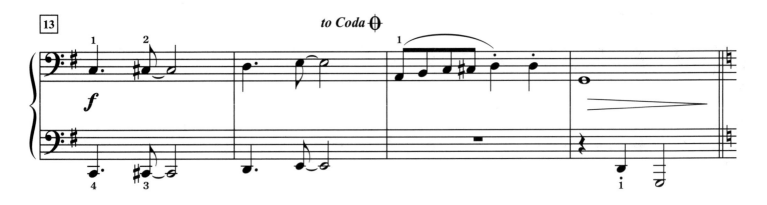

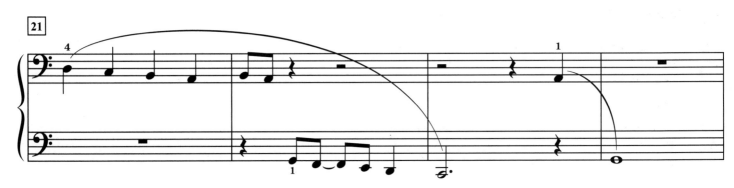

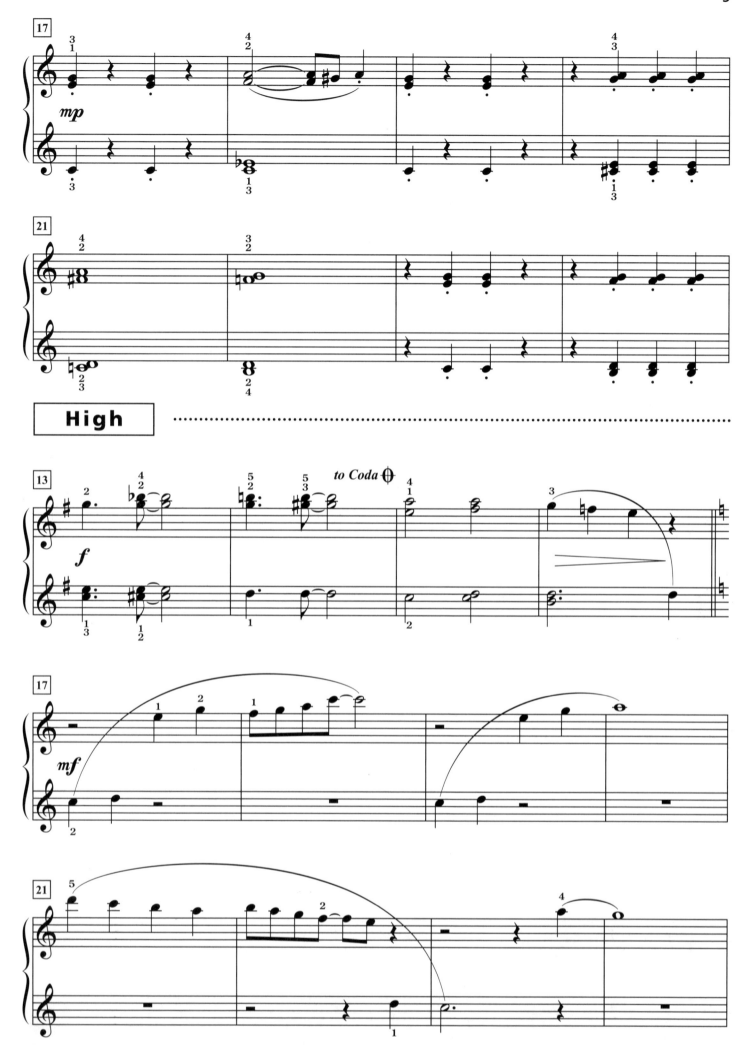

Middle

Low

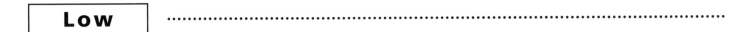

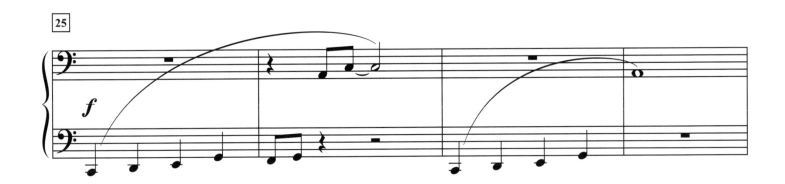

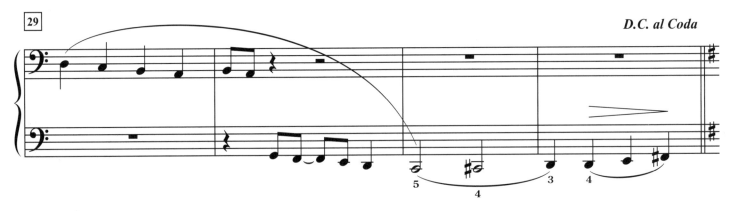

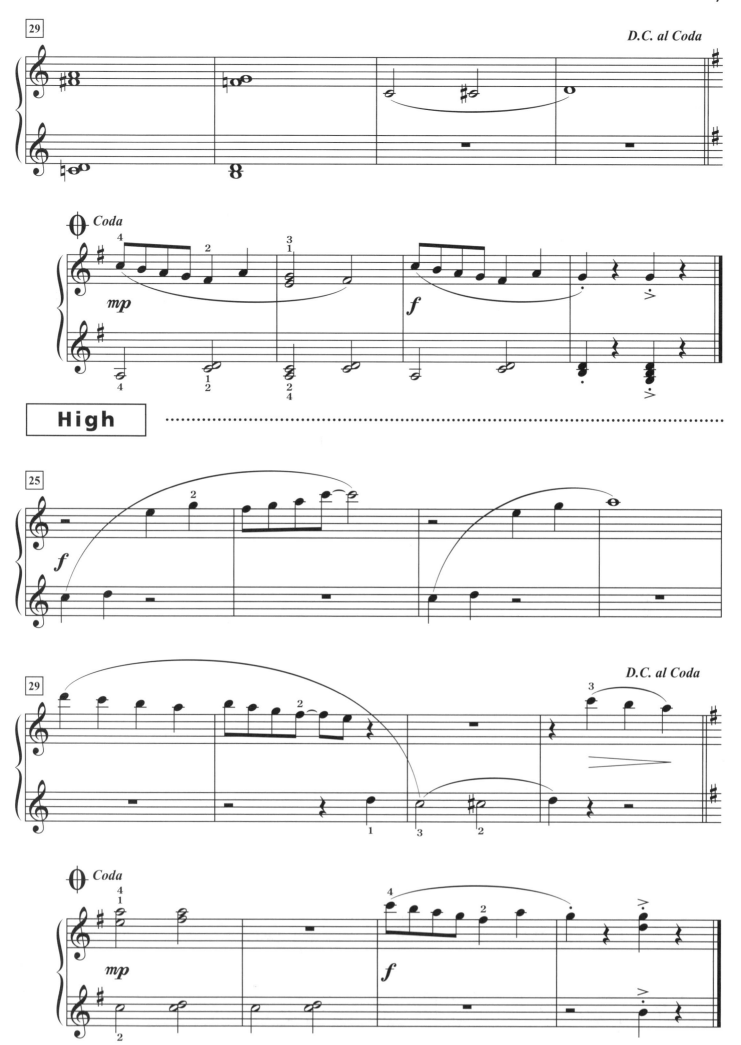

Irish Circle Dance

Melody Bober

Middle

Low

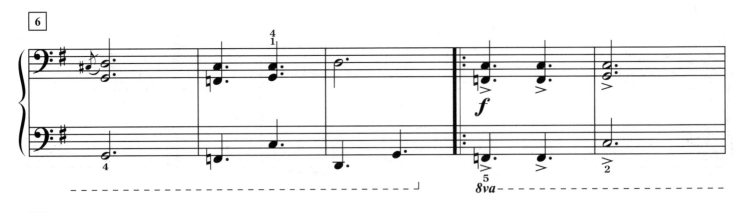

Middle

Low

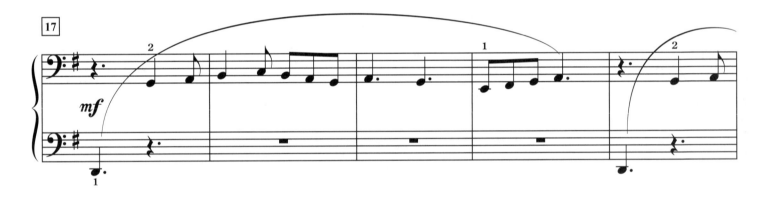

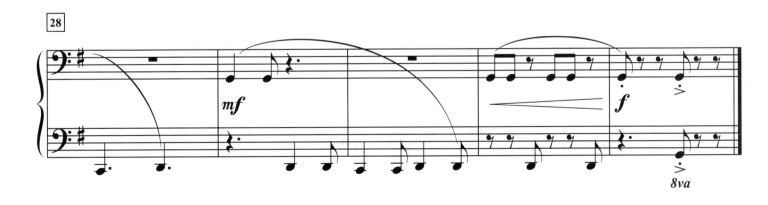

8va

High

Snap, Clap, Boogie

Melody Bober

Middle

Moderately fast, snappy (♩ = 116)

Low

Moderately fast, snappy (♩ = 116)

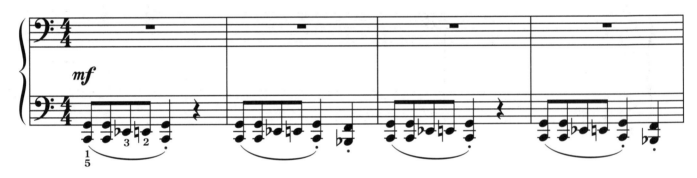

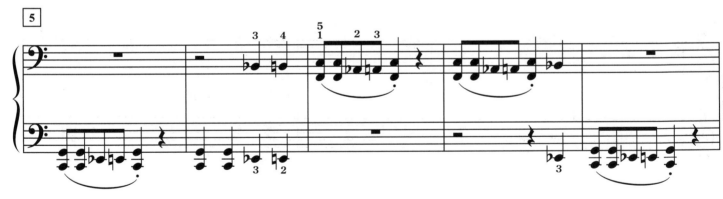

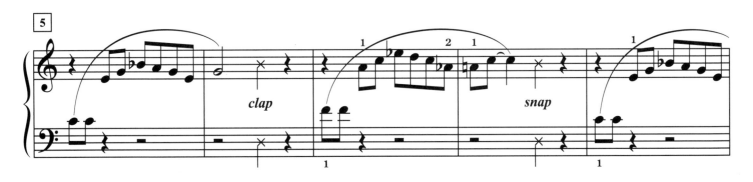

High

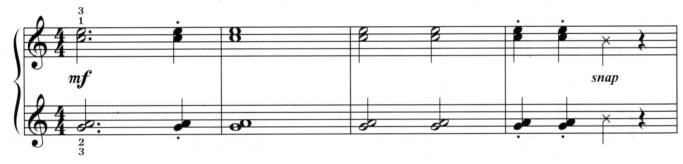

Moderately fast, snappy ($\quarternote$ = 116)

Both hands one octave higher throughout

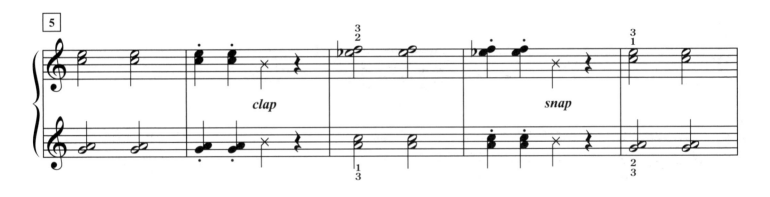

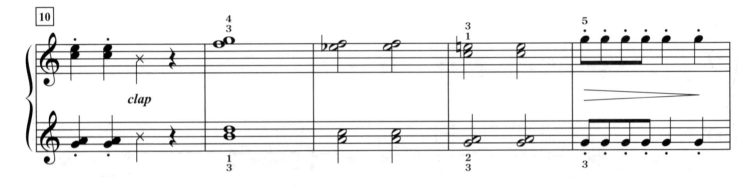

Middle

Low ....

High

Middle

Low

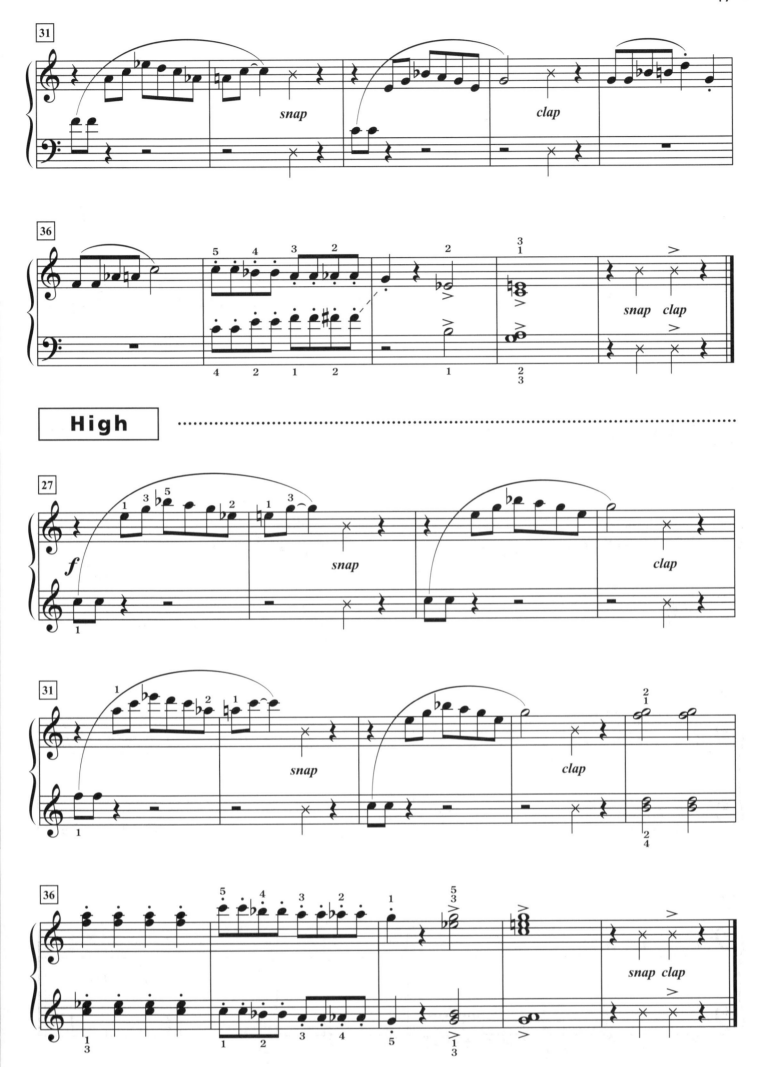

Unsolved Mystery

Melody Bober

Middle

Moderately fast, suspenseful ($\quarternote = 104$)

Low

Moderately fast, suspenseful ($\quarternote = 104$)

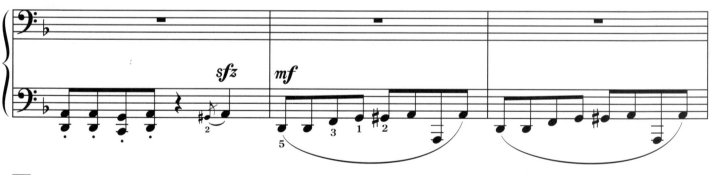

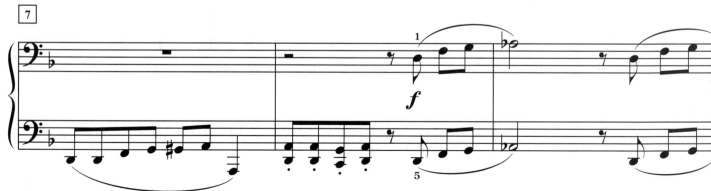

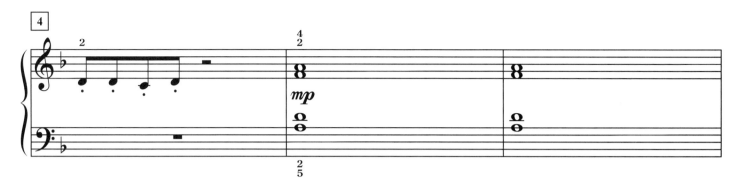

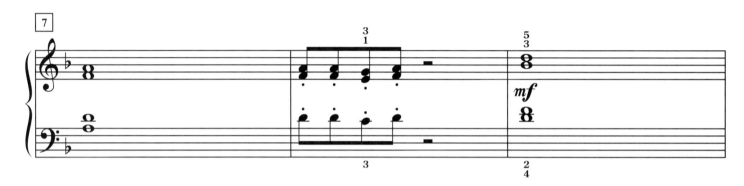

High

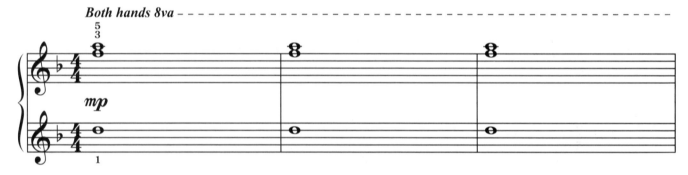

Moderately fast, suspenseful ($\quarter = 104$)

Both hands 8va

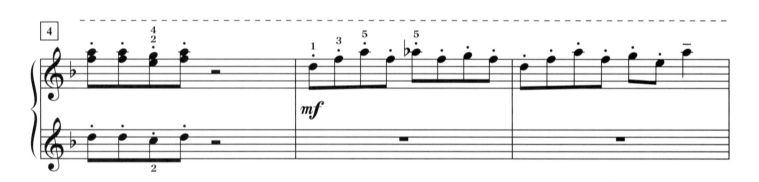

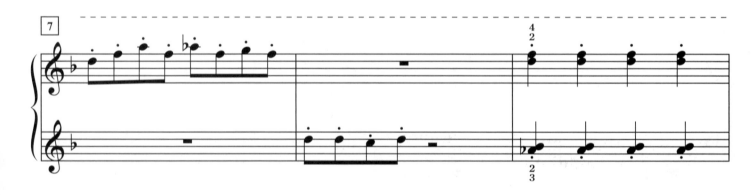

Middle

Low ....

8va –

High

Middle

Low

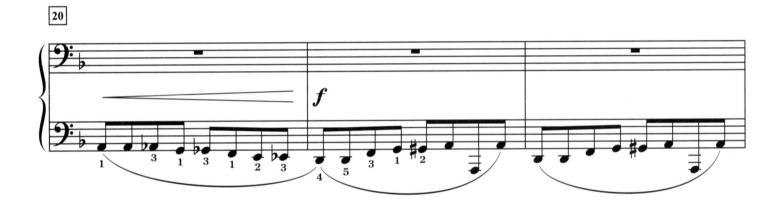

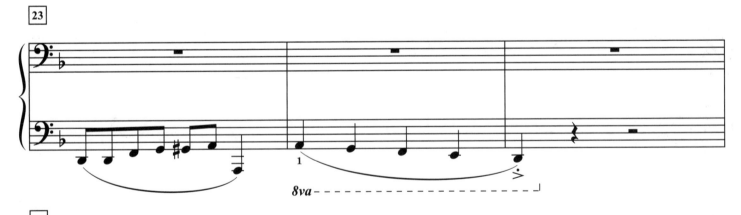

High

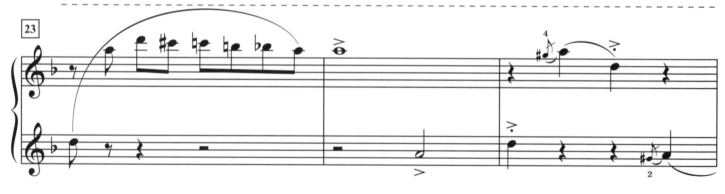

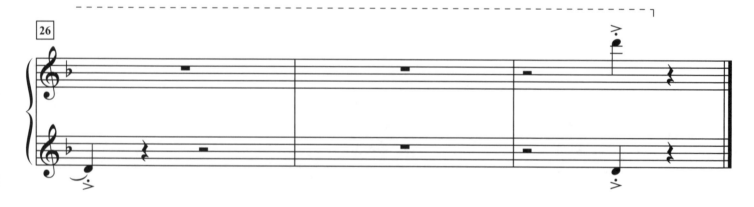